OCEAN LIFE

Adult Coloring Book

Lee Rupprecht

"Waving, Washing, Turning, Churning –
the waves of Life are continually in motion".

The Ocean is filled with an enormous amount of life; plants, animals, fish, crustaceans, algae, and more.

There are a variety of ocean habitats where life can survive and thrive; intertidal zones, sandy shores, rocky shores, mudflats, mangroves and salt marshes, estuaries, kelp forests, sea grass meadows, coral reefs, surface waters, deep sea, vents and seeps, trenches, and seamounts.

New discoveries are found everyday within and upon the ocean.

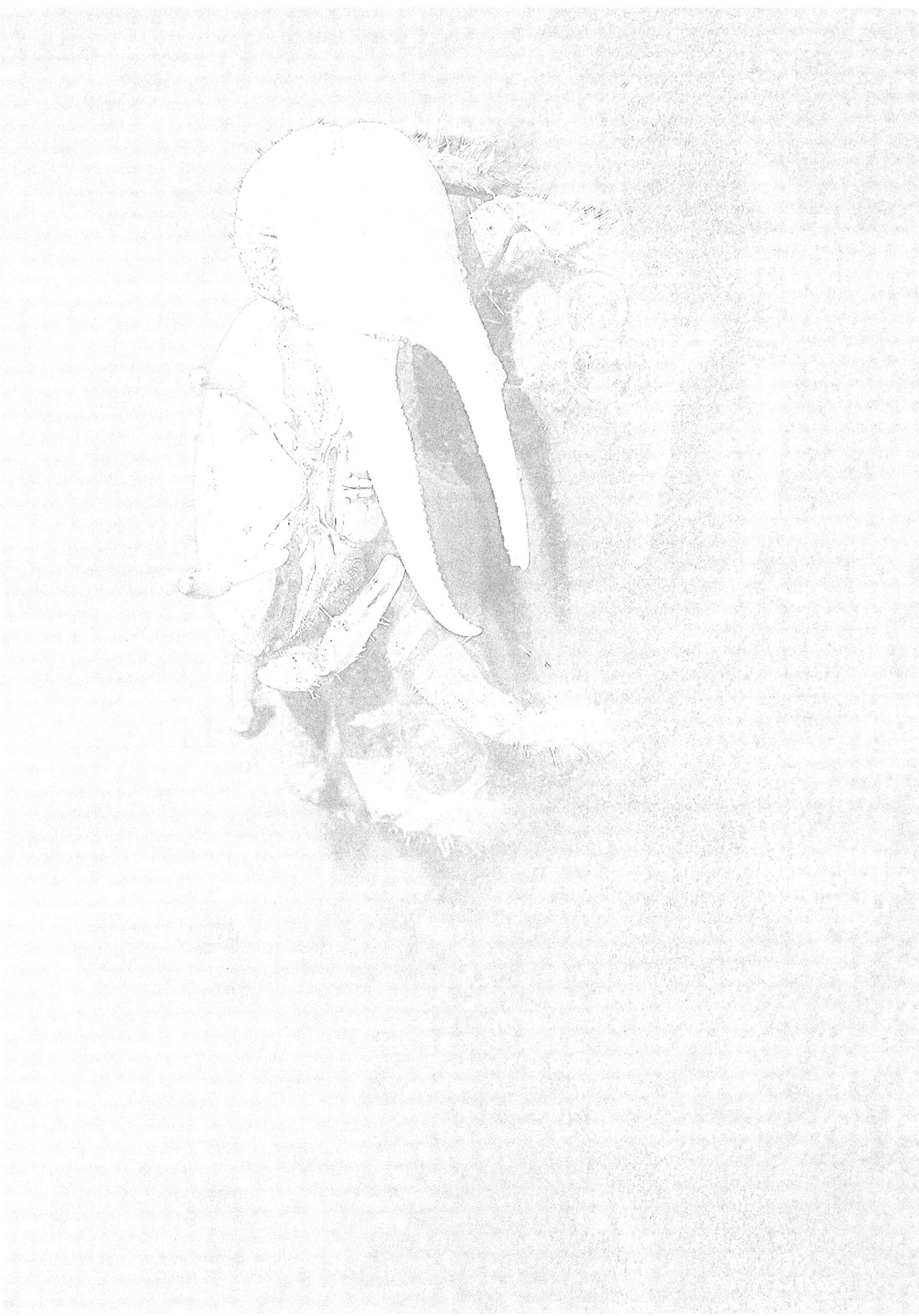

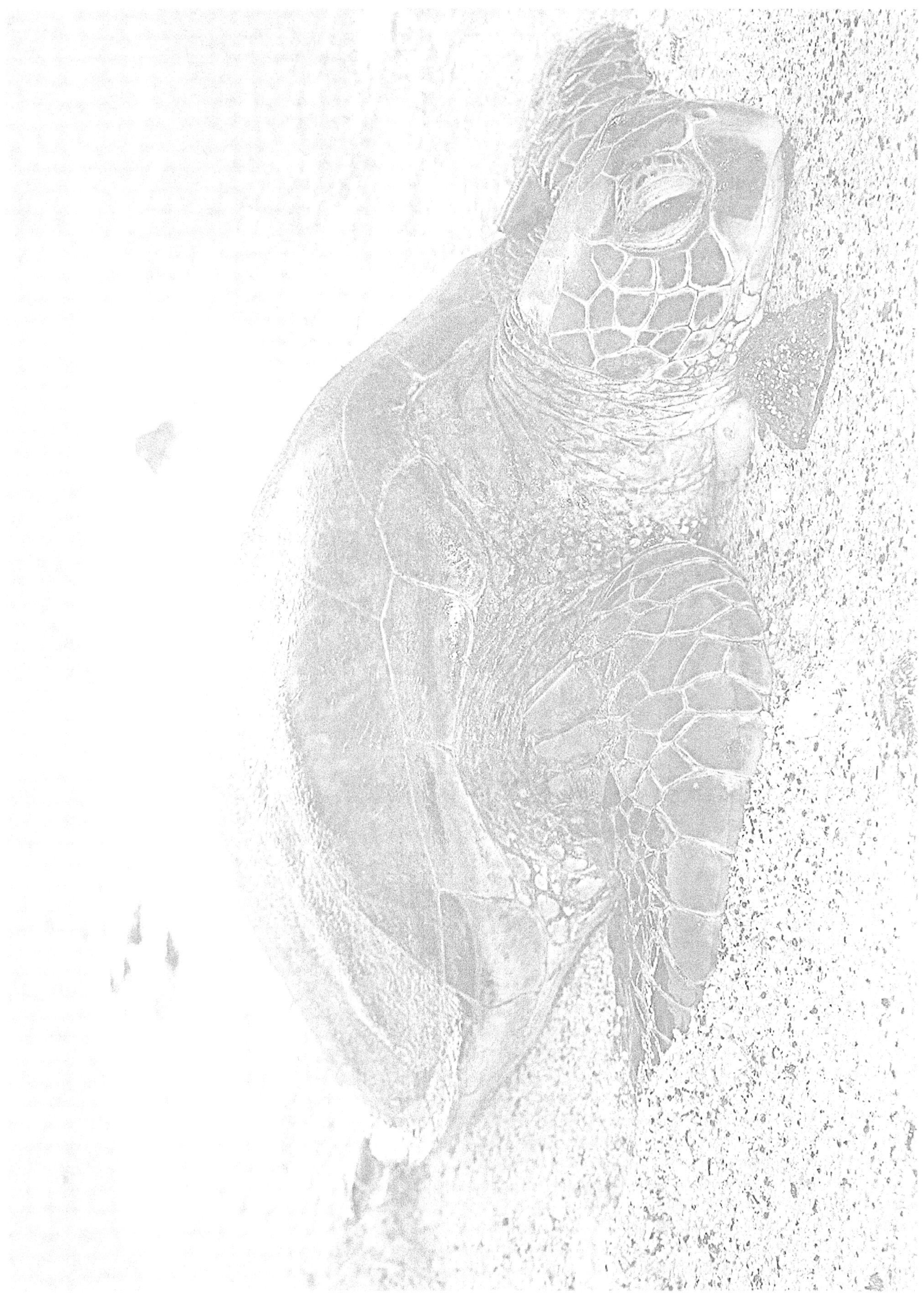